Sara,
Enjoy the book!
RG

Copyright © 2015 by Rosalind D. Guy

Chasing Rainbows Publishing trade paperback edition 2015

Printed in the United States of America
Original cover image by Jasmine Leigh Guy

Author's Note

I've never believed in fairy tales. Not even as a little girl. I've known for as long as my memory stretches back that there is no such thing as "happily ever after." I remember things like standing around with friends in the apartment complex where I lived, talking about the six-year-old little girl whose mother would allow drug dealers to have sex with her daughter in exchange for crack cocaine. I remember the popsicle man who drove through the apartment complex every day, looking to serve up something more than frozen confectioner's treats. I remember wondering why my brother's dad touched me differently when my mother was away at work. And I remember how even the park next to the apartment complex wasn't a safe place to go alone because it was supposed to be home to a "monk man," who would hurt little kids.

So, no, I never believed in fairy tales. I never thought some Prince Charming or fairy godmother would show up one day and change my life so I could live happily ever after. Not even in my dreams did I allow such childish notions to take root in my soul.

But I have always believed in the power of love. I remember doing things to try and win my mother's love, which I thought I never had. I remember longing for love instead of material things. Love, I thought, would be easier to obtain. After many painful heartbreaks, I realized true love is almost as elusive as happily ever after. Still, I always wanted nothing more than to love and be loved.

So the poems in this book are all about love. Because I believe that every story is a love story. Someone either loves, feels unloved, feels incapable of loving, feels betrayed by love, feels unsure about what love is, is afraid to love…Everyone feels something about love. And that feeling has shaped them.

So, I offer you a love story told in the form of poems. The poems in this collection have been weaved together to offer you a love story that I hope will touch your soul as much as it has touched mine.

One of the most profound statements I've read about love came from the poet Rainer Maria Rilke in *Letters to a Young Poet*. Rilke said, "believe in a love that is being stored up for you like an inheritance and trust that in this love there is strength and a blessing, out beyond which you do not have to step in order to go very far." I believe and I hope that you do too.

Peace & Love,
Rosalind

Why I Sing the Blues

Feeling So Black & Blue

Big Bird Was Wrong

I used to think the world
was like Sesame Street.
We'd live and learn;
the lessons were always fun
and singing was fun too.
When you fell and got hurt,
an adult was there to make it better.

On Sesame Street,
adults didn't shove you down
or rape you,
thugs didn't
blast up your porch
with AK-47s,
and you didn't get robbed
or beaten for simply existing.

On Sesame Street,
your parents loved you,
your friends did too.
Sesame Street
was a great place to be.
And the songs you sang
didn't rise from a life
of loneliness, pain or shame.

Big Bird made you believe
that life was fair.
Bert and Ernie made you believe
the most important lesson
was to learn to share.
So, where do you learn to
duck and dodge,
to steal from your brother
or even your mother?
Where do you learn
the difference between crack and coke,
how to take your first smoke?
Where do you learn that nothing matters
but clothes, shoes and bling?
On my street; those are the lessons
you learn on my street.

The Streets Are Not Always Paved with Gold

The streets are not always paved with gold and
if you knew what they really were paved with
it just might make you sick   to know
that the streets sometimes are paved with
other people's spit and so much other shit.
Some can turn their eyes away and ignore it
but that's no easy feat, to ignore the stench of shit
littering the streets especially when you're forced
to live with it, all the shit you create and that's
created by other people, people just trying to find gold
at the end of the rainbow.

In the ghetto – I think that's what they call it now,
the streets are littered with bloody sacs leaking
under-formed fetuses and bloody memories of
unfulfilled dreams and shitty diapers and
broken glass from the cheap beer winos use to
chase away those childish things like
trying to achieve the American dream because
poverty and no opportunity work hand-in-hand in
the land of the free and the home of the brave
to ensure some people, without a doubt, will die
never having lived beyond their own meager and
insufficient means. And no childish gleam
in eyes cloudy with the residue of truth
can dilute this dose of reality.

Haven't you heard it said that
the streets are not always paved with gold?
There's so much shit the streets can hold
shit no one can identify or label
anymore
besides who the hell tries
anymore?   Too much effort required
so we train ourselves to
step over the shit littering our streets
like crackheads and corporate thugs and
regular old thugs, the young and old.

So when little Johnny walks outside his
house ---- hold the hell up
what you mean "little Johnny?"
His pigmentation darker than mine so I,
I'll call him John
'cuz old John was a travelin' man and
Shouting John hold my mule while
Old Big-Eyed John is long gone, but
before he left he said that "If a man die,
he will live again."
So, yeah, I think we'll call him John.

The streets are not all paved with gold.
Hell, some people don't even got
they streets yet, 'cuz they so busy buying
Michael Kors and Louis Vuitton,
racking up receipts and ain't got time to notice
they traveling on dirt roads that take them thru
the back woods and gutters that lead to
hell.

But, at least they look nice right?

B sides y u need a strt wen u
ain't goin' nowhere special?
All you tryna do is cop
the newest Jordan shoes and buy
the bag that's in season 'cuz it's
more than a sin 2 B caught
not matchin' everyone else
with they million dolla dreams
and penny man schemes to
fake the funk and look rich
even tho you ain't got shit 2 eat.

The streets not always paved with gold
especially when you got to travel
500 years to get from plantation to
hell to penitentiary to final resting
place and never once get to see ---
Happy-go-lucky Boulevard or
Dream Big Street 'cuz
you got to cross
Keep a Positive Attitude Highway
down by Route 17 and
yo shoes got holes in them so
you just stay where you are
and steal little pieces of happiness
when you can. You can then blame the man
instead of the system, a broken system
held together by the rusted chains of
racism, sexism, colorism, ageism and
apathy –ism dressed up in swag gear.

Don't you know the streets not always
paved with gold? There's so much shit
littering the streets that
sometimes all you wanna do is sit in yo
house, watch TV and let other people
do the thinking for you. Sometimes it seems it
ain't even worth trying when you know
the streets are not always paved with gold.

Wake Up

Roll Call:
Thirteen year old shot and killed Saturday afternoon
Titania Mitchell, Jacksonville

Fourteen year old gunned down after leaving party
Justin Thompson, Bridgeport

Fourteen year old girl gunned down while at park
Hadiya Pendleton, Chicago

Fifteen year old killed by off-duty cop
Justin Thompson, Memphis

Sixteen year old killed during "alleged" home burglary
Cleveion Coley, Memphis

Seventeen year old shot while waiting for bus
Johnathan Johnson, Nashville

Eighteen year old mother shot and killed
Janay McFarlane, Chicago

Somebody better shake you
up. Wake you up to reality.
Old whitey's not tryna
take away yo civil rights
no mo. 'Cuz what's civil about
colored children killing each other
over colors that belong to the rainbow

after a violent storm —we thought it would
wash all our sins away, but it brought
them to dock in our own back yards.
And what's civil about grandpa
squeezing a leg underneath the
dinner table, a lurid reminder of
the exchange of fluids that will take
place later on? What's civil about
a toddler perishing in the flames of
his mother's neglect?

Don't you see, in the face of reality,
a need to wake up for a change?

The seeds of civility were planted
forty-five years ago and watered
with fresh blood —I AM A MAN—
and yet only a fistful of flowers bloomed,
not enough to fill the world
with vibrant petals and inviting scents
so profound, no lines of poetry
would be able to contain them.
Instead, the streets are filled with
the coppery scent of blood and
the all-too familiar essence of
post-coital, incestuous, and carnal
pleasures. The air is peppered with
the scent of bloated corpses and
forgotten and lost and wandering souls.

So, wake up, yeah man I'm talkin' to you
Wake up! 'Cuz nobody's chasin' you,

tryna keep you from opening a book
even to steal one look inside and see
how it's possible to soar with both feet
on the floor. Ain't nobody tryna keep you
from holding your family together —don't
blame the auction block no more,
'cuz it's all on you.
Wake up! Boys and girls and see
this is a brave new world.
If you would only wake up,
you would see the enemy, for he
now looks like you and me.
So, wake up and when you look
in the mirror, you'll finally see
a slave master who's hidden deep within.

The Paper Bag Life

People look at me and just shake
they head. They say, "I don't understand
why you want to live like this. You
need to get a job, then you can have all I have."

They cut me down with words and leave
me feeling bad. I don't ever respond, except
inside my head, "I ain't got no real purpose
in life, if that's what you mean."

When people look at me, I know all they
really see is the paper bag quality of my
soul, wanting only to have me crumple up
and die or just disappear completely. They paint me
as a paper bag 'cuz I look nothing like them
in my beat up shoes and dirty jeans.

"We need to eat," my stomach growls up
at me; it doesn't seem to comprehend
that paper bag people not expected to
want to eat, so it keeps screamin' at me.
How can I explain to my gut that it ain't
easy bein' seen as a throw-away man, living
what most people see as a worthless life.

My family gets a check for me; they s'posed

to provide for me and take care o' me, but they choose
instead to rest in the lap of luxury and frivolity
and my stomach becomes their mortal enemy.
Ain't nobody tryna feed me when they need to get
the latest fashionable jeans and the flyest kicks.

Days will pass and fold into each other before
I can pay my stomach to shut the fuck up.
And even then, I can hear the dissatisfied grumbles
making they way up to me. But what the hell you
want from me, I'm just the paper bag man.

But this one day, within the sanctuary of that
pissy-smelling toilet stall, with the toilet that's
overflowing with the feces of life, I got down on my knees
and let the Lord and my stomach speak to me
as if I was not a paper bag man, but just me. A man.

Out in the heart of that restaurant lobby, a woman
and her little family were getting ready to sit down
and eat. She passed right by me, without looking at me
so a quarter was all I could bring myself to ask for.
I didn't want to become a burden so she'd treat me
like my family does; I wanted to slink away unnoticed
but, man, oh man, I needed to eat.

Standing at that crossroads, knowing I needed food to eat,
I vomited the contents of my paper bag life, trying
desperately to explain why my life seemed to be steeped

in triviality – why I was living the paper bag life.

Most people think I ask, not beg-
cause I'm definitely no beggar- them to feed me
so I can take the money and feed an addiction
that's sustaining me, induce a medicated coma
to make bearable this paper bag life, but,
in actuality, I just want to eat.

And, that woman, when she finally did look at me
I could finally see the light, 'cuz she saw me
the way I used to see me, and only sometimes see
myself when I have the ability to look clearly at myself
in the grimy mirrors and broken glass littering the
alleyways.
And, I thanked God for leading me to the one who
wouldn't see the half man I see in the broken bottles
and discarded trash in my home, the alley. She didn't
see just another throw-away man, but

just a man who needed a meal, something to keep
my stomach from cursing me with the undeniable
uncertainty of leading a paper bag life, where eating
becomes a luxury and living becomes the destiny of
only those with money, while

men like me bear the inevitability of becoming
scraps of men littering the streets and parks and
alleys 'cuz sometimes it's just impossible to

get the money for a place to stay or food to eat.
So, you know, people like me stop counting

No money to count
No family to count on and
Considered no account in society.

The People Beneath the Street

What the hell u talking bout
down there, he yelled at the

ground. People stopped to stare
at him & to judge him crazy.

People are living in the sewers
and we're too crazy to notice.

Even when we hear the low rumble
of voices coming from beneath the street,

we'll do our best to ignore them
because we're afraid of being called crazy,

so we march zombie-like through
the streets like simple-minded sheep

being led to the slaughter, trying not to
appear crazy and ignoring the

voices of the people beneath the street.

*Dedicated to those among us who are open to a reality
that causes others to call them crazy. We're crazy for not
wanting to be different, but you're more crazy for being
okay with being different. Right? Right.

You Say You Wanna Be Free

u say u wanna b free
    then
drag the slave ship into ur
      back yard 4 some black-
      on-black criminality

u say u wanna b free
    then
drag the slave ship into the
back alleys 4 shoot 'em up
dealing 4 self or anybody

u say u wanna b free
    then
u drag the slave ship into
ur bedroom, use it 2 crush
ur lover, friend, wife.
ur black fists   a weapon
of domestic brutality

u say u wanna b free
    then
u drag the slave ship 2
the middle of the street
where u beat ur neighbor
2 within an inch of life

4 parking on the strt nr ur
fresh new ride
but u wanna b free, right?

Shake that shit off,
drop those chains of
the slave mentality u
keep draggin' around ---
stop --- focusing only on the
bones at the bottom of the
seas & oceans –
what about the bodies
in the   middle of the street?

Sparky's Is Gone

Sparky's Gulf Grill doesn't stand where it used to.
It has been eclipsed by moon pies that are flavored
with the careless nature of a love gone stale. And
that's why I was there that day. My friend said to me
       Well, maybe if you remove the crust
from around the edges, it'll be fine. If you toast it,
it's done though. What does she really know
about toast and moon pies or that forever look
I saw in *her* eyes – I struggled to describe it to my friend.

Destruction glimmered in my friend's eyes. Not the kind
that destroys, but the kind that *kills* despair.
And I
came to the counter to order a drink. You remember
it, right? It wasn't dark yet. I could still see sunlight.
Maybe if you'd only known that my heart was broken.
Brown skin doesn't suit everyone, so if I rub
my brown skin on you, let me assure you that
it (my skin or my color) doesn't rub off that easily. You see,
I didn't really want a drink. I ordered one so you wouldn't
judge me. Then you cringed to touch me.
And my quarter and dime soared down to my palms
on wings of indifference to change.

One day I was riding my bike, a blue Schwinn,
when I was about nine or ten. I fell and scraped
my knees and the insides of my hands. My knees

turned from brown to red and my palms turned brown
from the dirt and silt on the ground. That's the
only time brown and white touch and rub off.

But I guess you never owned a Schwinn. If I could do it
again
I'd give you the space and the time to understand that
giving up on love was the only sane thing I've ever done.
And that nothing, and I repeat nothing, would ever force
me to try and defend the color of my skin or my love for
him.

Man on the Eleventh Floor

A man killed himself
today. I didn't try to stop
him. I watched him climb
out onto the ledge outside
his window, knowing he was just
trying to be free. His drastic
actions made mockery of the
grief that was binding me. I knew he
was trying to show me that
I didn't have to be wound up
in the continuum of confusion
that was eating away at me. I
could have screamed, up at him,
told him we all want to be free, but
I mimicked his actions as I stood
below, a mime in the tragi-comedy
of me and he, lives that became
intertwined in that moment. When he
began to move along toward the
shadows, trying to escape the light
of the moon, I only moved to
follow where he would lead, all
the while pondering how it would be
to swim in his eyes, dark pools of
sadness, no misery. Sadness can be
caught in the breeze by a coincidental
smile, a heavenly cacophony of
angel wings that conspire to embrace

the one who is sad, but misery roots
deep into the soul and flowers into
something so dark, we spend years
trying to break free, only to find the
chains refusing to leave. Still his eyes
held me mesmerized, made me wish
it was sadness there and not misery
because maybe we could meet
for coffee one day and free each
other. I didn't try to stop him.
There was no logical reason to
explain the slow build of anger
I felt as I watched the disintegration
before me, the resignation to be free
doomed us both. Angry bile rose up
in me and drowned all the words
I could think to say, to stop him, to
save me. I swallowed my anger and
turned and walked away. A man
killed himself today. And I can't
explain why I didn't try to talk him
out of it and I didn't stop to cry
when I finally knew the feeling of
stepping out on the wings of a prayer
unsaid, thinking I had wanted to
save him, to save me, when all I'd really
wanted was to be able to pass by.

Love Letter #3

The morning rays caress your skin
like dew on the grass before daybreak,
of a new day, a new beginning.

I reach to touch you, but I am distracted
by the light I breathe, when I dream, of your
presence and it causes something to shift
in me.

Your smile, your smell, your taste, your touch and
your voice take me to a place where memories of us
portray vivid thoughts, thoughts as airy and free
like the light I breathe when I think of loving you.

So please take this opportunity to take in
the light I breathe when you lay in my arms
to rest your heart and soul for eternity,
an eternity created for only you and me.

*I found this letter among the things you left behind. I sat
on the floor and cried for hours after finding it. I wish you
had taken this with you, carried it away with your love.

My Heart Bleeds

My heart bleeds
4 the daughters who
I didn't birth naturally,
no bruised flesh birth &
no swollen feet birth &
no stretch marks birth &
no result of being fucked birth.

I birthed them thru
the words I created
4 them.
Words 2 tell my daughters
how I came 2 love them
when
I didn't birth them or
nurse them.

Sometimes I wanna
scream & holler 4 all
the shit my daughters
have 2 go thru.

When I hear how u
beat my daughter so u
wouldn't feel less a man;
u left her crumpled
&

with the blues flowing thru her veins:
questioning how u can luv her
when
u leave her so black & blue.

I just wanna scream at u
how fuckin' dare u
put ur hands on her   me   she
2 do anything but luv her   me   she
when we deserve to B treated
oh so carefully   so
don't u dare put ur
hands on me   her   she
2 smash me   her   she
in the face—SMASH it,
that's what u say when
u have ur woman ur way
so
why r we surprised when
u don't view us as a prize
but as a trophy 'cuz
clearly there's a difference.

I'm not tryna B mean
but dammit
how dare u let that
motherfucka touch ur
daughter in that way,

the way only her husband
should know her, not ur
husband or baby daddy or
just him.

&

My heart bleeds
when I think of the things
our daughters do 2 try &
B free 2 indulge in childish
things like straight hair weaves,
big butt cheeks hanging out of
daisy duke jean shorts & being free
2 sleep with whomever she pleases
'cuz "if you please," it's my business
who I sleep with. It just makes me wanna
scream 2 see my babies this way,
but u don't seem 2 B able 2 see
that shit do stink
when our girls think
they were created to take
care of others while no one
takes care of them, to be abused
while no one protects them &
my heart bleeds 'cuz I wanna
protect them all, and hell, I

wanna B the one 2 tell them
"I love you girl, so lean on me."
But, first, I'm gonna need
someone 2 be there 4 me
so
until then I guess my heart will
continue 2 bleed 4
the daughters I didn't give birth
2
& that includes me.

Daddy

Daddy! Stop Daddy!
You said it wouldn't hurt,
oh Daddy, it does.

I Wasn't Born a Junkie

I wasn't born a junkie.
It's just one of those things
I fell into, like love & madness.

Sucking on the end of a
crack pipe, a substitute for
cradling a thickly veined penis
between my lips, sucking & slurping
like a cone spewing forth ice cream.

Taking a deep breath,
I have to relax before it
enters me. The smoke rushes
forward, grabs me
by the neck, then sets me free.

Adrift on a smoke-filled sea,
enveloped in a sublime haze;
an attempt to escape the misery
I have created for myself.

I pull the plastic tool back
from my lips. I just have to see
for myself the lovely smoke as
it fills me, forces my lungs to expand.

The pleasure leaves me feeling complete.

Inhale death, exhale life & push away memories-
the Holy Trinity.

The feeling is only fleeting.
Eventually my lover must leave.
He will get dressed quickly and
it'll almost seem as if he was never
there; that is until he comes again.

It started as an innocent game
a game that, in fact, had no name.
the object of the game was to run
and hide and my uncle would turn
his head, pretend to look away.
He always knew, though, just where
to find me. It was easy for him.
I always hid in the exact same place
I went to my bed, hid under the covers,
thought to myself, "I'm really clever."

Folded into the darkness underneath
my covers, I first took his penis in
my mouth. It was like eating candy,
that's what my uncle told me. This
was a game all our own, our very own
little secret, nobody to share the shame.

I wasn't born a junkie. It was a gift
bestowed to me by a friend who knew

that little boys have a very hard time
acknowledging that naiveté and
my uncle stole my virginity. In exchange
for my virginity, they gave me reality
covered in a sperm-colored bow,
a ribbon of eternity to avoid looking
in the mirror to see
the trail of tears mixed with semen,
the only remembrance for me
that really matters.

I wasn't born a junkie.
It was a gift bestowed to me.

One Man's Love

His love was a butcher
knife to my soul, killing me
& destroying my self
                    l
                        o
                            v
                                e

Brother Man

Brother man thought he was slick with hiz pick-up
line. The brother walked right up to me and

committed the ultimate no-no deed. He
fingered the kinky locks of my 'fro like I was

some Korean hair store ho. Wearing a steely gaze,
I tried to put him in his place, told him he needed to

step out my face 'cuz where he was headed,
he was going alone. The notes he was playing

with those slick ass words could never complement
my song. *Blues of a love junkie,*

a junkie for love. Tho there's no denying that's
exactly what I am, it wasn't enough anymore

to make me fall so low and settle for just another
relation-shit, more of the shit I'd dealt with while

trying to glue together pieces of my pain,
pain from the past and now pain from the present.

Oh you one of those bougie azz broads, he
said, you think you better'en me huh.
I looked at that fool who was wearing $300

tennis shoes, and pants that sagged so low,
I saw his vision for where he wanted to go.
The tags hung off the $150 Polo shirt & matching
jacket, black. He pointed his finger at the crown
of my 'fro & said we two sides of the same coin.

Then he looked down at my no name kicks and
my jeans so old there were rips in the knees.
A smile spread across his oily little face as
he composed his slickest line to date:
"Hey lil mama. Don't be like that. I just want
to be your special friend. You can be Lois Lane
and I'll be your Superman." I shook my head and
said, "I hate to let you down but I ain't looking
for no damn clown that goes running from place
to place, leaving no time to finish a race or put
down roots 'cuz he always trying to save the human
race. I need a man who sees only me and a
man who likes what he sees when he looks at
me, so he knows not to waste time trying to
fix me. And, by fix me, I mean get me to be more
like him. 'Cuz you see, my brother, I already know
that I am a gem. I need no polishing, refining or
saving. I just need a man who wants to stay
with me and only me." I must admit, my rhyme
left him looking confused and not the least
bit amused.

So, I broke it down for him. A band-aid, I told him,

never takes the place of skin. It conceals the pain, keeps it within and allows for the healing while doing the concealing. Once that sticky little strip of healing cloth has picked up bits of crusty blood and pus and other stuff, it becomes nothing but trash. And what, my brother, do you do with your trash?

Brother man just shrugged like I was playing a game and said, "One man's trash is another man's treasure." That smile of his stretched nearly a mile ass wide, but I had something for him that he wasn't expecting. "I'm nobody's band-aid," I said with a smile, I'm not here just as a cover 4 ur broken heart and lonely nights, so I can become the concealer for your broken ass life. Coming to me to get quick pick-me-ups like a crackhead in an alley, down on his knees to suck the drug dealer's dick, just so he can forget what he has to face day by day. 'Cuz it's apparently easier to hide in the margins of society, while wishing to be free, hoping

one day that someone will show up to save you. Until then, you drop rhymes on me like you can be my savior and hero, when we both already know, baby boy, it's not me who needs saving, it's you. But you too fearful to move, so you stand on the corner

spouting tired ass moves, stick and move,
duck and dive, while not opening your eyes
to see the reality that's staring you deep
in your eyes. Well, I ain't got time for that.
I got one life to live and I ain't wasting it
by being no damn band- aid for some man
who too damn weak to walk away from
what makes him unhappy while filling my mind
with castles in the air and I wanna take u there
while u tryna keep up with fools who think
living is existing, just making it from day to day
while tryna accumulate enuf dough to
stay fresh.

Death Sleeps With One Eye Open

Death lurks, shrouded in
darkness, aggrieved by the
patience of waiting. Death

knows few among us will
lift the veil, search for fear
in the eyes of death. Shake

death to its insecure
core. So death stands
taller each day, believing

one fear traded for another
equals strength. There

is unspoken certainty that
all who live shall look upon
the face of death. Death

keeps one eye open. Waiting,
waiting for the moment when
death can seize upon you. Kill

you without a fight. So when
death barely taps you on the
shoulder, it's a sign that death

is not prepared to embrace
the fullness of your life, Yet.

Choosing instead to offer a gentle
reminder of his existence like
an insecure lover. Death

sometimes craves attention
and the assurance that you and
I have not forgotten, and

to remind us whenever we do
finally want him, he'll be there
waiting in the shadows. Death.

Just waiting.

You're Just 13

Maybe it really is an
unlucky number, 13.
You're just 13, you
should be running across
football fields, chasing
little girls, magnifying ants
on top of an anthill, or just
lying on your back staring
at the clouds as they pass
by, wondering how life will
be when you're older, more
than 13. The only dust you
should be eating should
come from racing your
buddy down the block and
over the hill when he
challenges you to a foot race
through the neighborhood. But,
it's the hood though
that placed a monster inside
your belly. And we all know
monsters never stay hidden
for long. The monster in you
laid dormant just three years
'cuz at three years old you
shoved your little brother
down a flight of stairs and
stabbed your dog in the eye

with a crayon – no one told you
to use those crayons to color
your world and see more than
just black and white and sometimes
gray. The monster grew and grew,
consuming you and everything you
touched. Then at five years old, you
grabbed a pair of scissors and tried to
stab your teacher and it became time out
for the madness that overshadowed your
mom's sadness when she began to
recognize the monster growing
in you. She took you to a doctor
recommended by a friend of a friend,
and that doctor made you dazed &
confused with medications used
to take down lions and bears;
the glass in your eyes blinded all
who saw you 'cuz
they no longer recognized you
so they stopped trying to tame
the monster inside 'cuz even a fool
knows pills don't kill monsters.
Do you keep Tylenol at the foot
of your bed to keep monsters from
filling your head with thoughts of
killing your family and friends? No,
it takes more to slay the demon within.
Warrior Mother Earth supplies her

children with the courage to slay
demons and keep them from slaying
her children, but when Mother Earth
has been raped and violated and beaten,
she forgets how to equip
her children, how to care for
her children, how to provide
her children with tools to
survive and thrive in a
world that crumbles brown
children and uses their broken
lives to sweeten their morning
bowl of cereal. Fruit Loops and
Honey Nut Cheerios taste better
sprinkled with the lives of
broken and battered children
who have monsters growing
in their belly. So, yeah, I think
thirteen really is an unlucky number.

Two Poets Died Today

Two poets died today and
at once the world fell silent.
No one spoke aloud about
the circumstances, but everyone
knew the poets both had died
in a multi-car pileup caused by
the crashing of their ideas.

The first poet to succumb to the
injuries he sustained called himself
a new revolutionary poet. In the days
before his demise, he'd been trying
to stir up a revolution amongst his
people. This revolution poet
sent up an SOS , saying we got to
learn how to help ourself. He said
we're not a Chinese toddler, but if you wanna
know the truth, nobody's coming to save us
either. We too have been left wallowing
in the blood of our ancestors, our peers,
all the blood that runs down the streets
and lands in the gutter.

Mr. Revolutionary was a straight up dude so
he wasn't prepared for the sucker punch from

Mr. Poet with an Attitude. That poet dude with a bad
attitude caused by the years and years of suffering
of his people in a place they were forced to call home.
Many days the poet with an attitude would walk down to
the beach and dance with spirits and corpses of the
ancestors who
perished under the thick blanket of water. Even without
knowing
about the future that awaited them, they knew
it would be nothing like what awaited them back home –
the real one—and so they swam toward the farthest shores
before giving way to the bottom of the ocean, the final
resting home that called out to them.

Death is not as permanent as slavery because the Master
of Death grants them the freedom to go to the poet when
he summons them, so every once and again
those spirits come up to dance with the poet dude with an
attitude. The movements serve as visual remembrances or
shared experiences, memories echoed in the deep, hollow
voice of the poet with a bad ass attitude.

In a voice so loud it shakes the foundation of the world,
the poet dude with an attitude calls his poet brother out,
labels him an Uncle, though most don't even consider him
a brother anymore. Poet dude with an attitude voices
the dissatisfaction of a people uprooted from the home
of their birth and transported to the home of their needs,

lands where they are forced to live as animals. Worse than animals who live in the zoo, who do nothing but lose their nature, the essence of their being, these people, said the dude with an attitude lose themselves entirely, locked not just behind physical bars, but mental bars that prevent them from thinking for themselves. Financial bars that keep them from moving up the corporate ladder while everyone stops to stare, but nobody ever stops to help.

In less than a minute, one poet finds himself on the ground and the other poet stands over him glowering and glowing with years of animosity and years spent trying to find himself,
but when he finally sees himself in the eyes of the revolution poet, he doesn't like what he sees, so he lashes out like the slave masters before him.

Bleeding from his mouth and nose, the revolution poet takes one last chance to lash right back at his foe. I love you brother, you should know. That's all this has ever been about. His words, genuine to be sure, hits the poet dude with an attitude right in the center of his chest, a hail of bullets
in the form of words. He too falls on the ground. Both lay there dying, no hero comes because poets are ignored unless their message is roses are red, violets are blue. So people step over them, pick through their pockets seeking

pieces of messages that were honey sweet to their ears and
then they kicked the poets where they lay
and that's why two poets died today.

Destruction

Destruction
gleamed in her
eyes, like the slicing
side of a hunting knife.

It was
obvious her hooded eyes
were looking for a
victim to slice apart.

No one
could understand
how her heart was breaking
or the choices she was making.
All they could see was the
destruction that gleamed
in her eyes.

Blood On My Hands

The ultimate betrayal

Sixteen years of tears
have not washed away
the stench of betrayal.
Brother against Brother,
or more accurately,
Sister against Brother.

I feel your blood on my hands.
It stains all I touch and
drips through my fingers when
I try to do my wash,
you know, cleaning
the laundry. Getting rid of
the dirty stains caused by
my living.

Blood stains the glass of
the mirror
in my bathroom,
covers my fingers like
shampoo as I wash
my short straight mane,
another lie,
mixes with the au jus

covering the roast I
serve to my family.

Bloodlust like truth
has its place
and always
makes itself known.

We
never gave you a chance
to have your voice during
your life
and death battle. So
you speak now. You
ask why. Why we chose
death without considering
your life?

Like back room criminals
we became, Mother and I
met the doctor outside,
far enough from earshot
though you already were asleep,
a sleep too deep
to shake you from. (I tried. I really did.)
Our back room deal
done,
we decided, us three,
to give up, decided

that nothing more
would be done
to save
you.

Cowards.
Afraid to face you
with the truth
that
you'd be dying soon
so
we
cheated you
out of your last days.

Shells of our bodies
stood by your side,
that small truth won't let me deny
that, in the end, we
abandoned you,
left you
alone
to try and understand the
things you were feeling and
the uncertainty of what was
to come. Death.

We had no answers
about the afterlife, still

the answers we did have
we kept guarded and
away from you.

We watched you withdraw
stop eating
stop living
stop caring and
we
retreated into a world of
illusive dreams more translucent
than hope, knowing that you
were still slipping through
our fingers, the sands of your life
clumped with the disease of our lies.

Sixteen years of tears
have not the power to
transport us back into time
for a re-do, so the
guilt is forever mine and
I will carry it always
hanging my head in shame
like you did when you
needed to know
what was going on with you.
But like the cancerous tumor
that invaded your body our
cancerous lies filled your mind

with darkness while we
watched you retreat further
into you, knowing you'd
eventually reach a point where
you'd never come back.

Untitled

As a young girl I would walk
along thin rails of abandoned
tracks near my home —the
loud blare ringing in my ears
trying to assure me, eventually
I'd know home. One day
the loud blare didn't make a
sound & the days weren't the
same. I stopped in the middle of
the road longing to hear the
metallic scream, a reminder
it was near. Silence was all
that came to me. A deep
fog of silence let me know
I was all alone.

It's a dangerous thing to
try & fill empty silence with
the noise of screams 'cuz
screams reverberate in emptiness
and fall on deaf ears. I can't
stop the memory of the screams
from keeping me up at night
so I sit in my home, still alone,
enveloped in a shroud of
darkness, listening for the
shrill screams. I want to

tell her to relax—make her
know that if she doesn't resist
it'll be all over soon.

The only problem I see is
I don't know if she's
screaming in my head or
if it's all happening in my
dreams. Is it the girl next
door who's screaming or
is the girl screaming really me?

Twisted Sister

Twisted sister twisted up in knots. People can't help but stare at your twisted knuckles on the hand that is gnarled and ugly from years spent washing and folding clothes for the white folk. Despite the pain that started in those twisted knuckles and radiated up your skinny arms –arms that had strength enough to carry load after load of dirty clothes – you would sit down every Sunday and pull baby girl into the cocoon of your legs. Every Sunday you greased her scalp, while braiding her hair 'cuz that style would last for a week at most. Giving your twisted knuckles time enough to heal so that you could do it all again next week.

Twisted sister sitting there with your stomach all in knots. Knots that keep you company as you wait on news from the doctor. Staring at your shoes in a shoebox sorta room, you await the words that could be your doom. To live or die? The word that he chooses to deliver to you will unwind or tighten your knots twisted sister. When the doctor saunters in the room, a folder in his hand, you want to wipe that smile off his face with the back of your twisted sister hand. Doesn't he know that you need to live, that you have four children depending on you? Twisted sister, whose husband left you behind – no, not for his secretary (what's that?), but for the woman who collects subway tokens Downtown. So you can't die now twisted sister.

Twisted sister, is that you I see through the open window wrapped up in a tangle of bed sheets. Those sheets all soiled with lovemaking that had nothing to do with love (AGAPE), but everything to do with low self-esteem that has you feeling a need to be stroked so that esteem can become engorged and fill all your empty places like that penis pretended to do last night. Your esteem yearns to be stroked and licked like your "spot," you know, the place behind your ear that when he touches it causes all your no's to melt into yeses and makes you think you're worth so much more. When you look down and see that swollen member, you tingle with self-satisfaction that leaves you thinking you're special and new, but, twisted sister, you need to know that he's dumping his low self-esteem into you, then leaving you a shitty mess. Twisted sister.

Twisted sister, why you sitting there watching your dreams spiraling down the drain of a fucked up reality not of your making; walking home that night how were you to know? You had no idea that the neighborhood creep would mistake you for a freak, taking your pussy and stealing it like it was a couple of ripe peaches from the neighborhood market. Oh my twisted sister, now you all alone staring at the wall, listening to that girl child in the other room, wondering if it will ever get better for you. My twisted sister, stop staring at the destruction planned for you by a fucked up

world that tried to spit you out and stomp on you. Go pick up that girl child and together you repair the twisted sister places that are threatening to overtake both of you.

Twisted sister, shh...you hear that twisted sister? That's the sound of a world trying to silence you. They want to know if you could stop being twisted sister 'cuz you killing the vibe of the carefree girl in a care-free world, where nobody cares that babies are getting their heads smashed in while mommas are living in sin and daddies are living alone, not even trying to repair their broken and twisted sisters. But there they go with those accusing eyes, begging you to untwist yourself so that you will stop hurting their eyes and will stop dirtying up their belief that this is a wide open world that offers the same promise of joy, love, and all that other good shit to us all. Twisted sister, I say to them, "Fuck you!" Now what about you twisted sister, what say you?

Headline

Black Man Shot and
Killed, a redundancy
to expose the complacency of
a lost generation.
A generation as off track
as a bad hair weave.

Teen Girl Kidnapped,
Raped, Beaten and
Forced to Prostitute Self.
Respect for women & girls'
bodies, long ago shelved
in favor of misogyny of
the female mind, body & soul.

Grandmother Stabbed, Grandson
Confessed. Alice Walker said it
best. As an elder, my
responsibility   to protect   care for
the young. Same young who
tore down the wall of respect to
stab granny in the chest so
they could have money jingling
to the tune of
We All Die Soon.

Young Child Left Alone in
Car, Store, Park, Home.
The cold arms of neglect
circling and tightening its grip
on his neck. No wonder
there are more kids
in the street, in the jail
taking the paved road to hell
'cuz the university side streets
seem out of reach when
you're left alone to find your own.
way. And, hell, you don't even know
what you supposed to be lookin' for.

Female Dog Trained to Fight.
Silly dog lost the fight, not
knowing her owner would
strip away her coat, her skin,
her dignity —all 'cuz she lost
a few dollars and now, to pay
for shoes for his kid,
he'll have to get a 9 to hmm....
Shit, dog, I ain't wanna work
for the man, so I make money
any way I can, but that damn dog
got her ass beat so bad, she
couldn't stand. Now I gotta go
stand in line for a white man's job
'cuz little Corey needs some new Jordans

and who the hell needs bread, when
they just released them new shoes?

Little Corey wuz up all nite so
he fell asleep in class. You
think he give a damn that
the principal judgin' the teacher
today? That bitch keep on
givin' him Fs and he almost
didn't get his new shoes. So
fuck them teachers, I gives 'em
the blues. Teacher Fired for
Mismanagement 'cuz she couldn't
control the kid who's out of control.
Sure, she could teach him to read &
all that other shit BUT that didn't
keep her from losing her job &
ending up on the breadline so
she can make some toast to go
with that jam the state, parents,
and administration put her in.

Black Man Shot and
Killed, a redundancy
to expose the complacency of
a lost generation.
A generation as off track
as a bad hair weave.

What is Black Power?

Black power is just an illusion that
has become an element of psyche delusion
when all the evidence of black power is
a black man in the White House, a man
who lacks any real power or desire to
do anything to help out those poor little
colored children who stood strong and helped
him knock down the back door, so he
could spend some time chillin' in the
White House.

Or is black power million dollar
heroes like Tiger, Kobe, or Jordan,
ball handlers who became millionaires
many times over and set a bar for swag –
cause that's what our children value –
with wearing the newest shoes cause
little Tommy might not know the answer to
2 times 2, but I guarantee you he knows exactly
when the new Jordans will be released.
Or maybe like Tiger, little Tommy thinks
the million handed to him for his ball handling skills
should be used to go on the prowl hunting for
a bunch of women for sale – make mine white
if you please – to show he too has
the rich white man's disease.

Maybe black power means making
million dollar heroes out of illiterate little boys
who spend all their money on expensive toys
to impress people who don't give a shit while
inspiring all colored children to want to be rich,
little boys who make millions by calling themselves
rappers and who allow the black women who
birthed them and loved them to be devalued with
labels like hoes, dime chicks, side chicks, and thots.
Or maybe black power means
not judging those same rappers too
harshly or holding them to any sort of
standard – cause you just jealous of "they success."
And ain't that some mess that success can
wear expensive clothing and shoes, eat in the
finest restaurants while some of their offspring
don't have shit to wear if it happens to be too
early in the week and mama can't wash, so
the kids wear the same shit over and over again. And
the only time Junior can hear daddy's voice is
by listening to that loud ass rap song that destroys
the beauty of us as a people.' Cuz daddy too busy
chasing that paper and getting high off success to
read to any of his illegitimate kids at night.

We sing rap lyrics like praise songs, rap
lyrics that defy simple principles of
unity and love for your brother while
glamorizing shooting your brother over

a dime bag or a dime chick or hitting a lick,
thinking the money will stick to your hands.
When in reality it'll all be gone too soon and
you nor your people will have a damn thing to
show for it. Black power today ducks and dodges,
like running from the police, the message of
lifting colored people out the streets
or sewers of life, keeping them from dragging
their foul-smelling selves into the nearest
Korean hair store, liquor store, Indian food store,
Chinese restaurant, or pawn shop to spend their
money & floss, not their teeth, but their style.

Black power, today, is sharing memes
about the latest black casualty, cause
"ain't it a shame," yet arguing for little Joe's
right to drop out of school, out of life for that matter,
and fall into a life of criminality cause killing
off our own soldiers is the way to prosperity
for our people. And complacency and apathy
have become the standard of normality for our
people. To make it is to have more dollars in the
bank than the next "nigga," not to invest in community,
trying to uproot the criminality that has become the
standard of living; read: our no snitch mentality and
willing acceptance of being clothed in ignorance of
the see no evil, report no evil mentality
that makes our 'hoods into war zones where
our own little colored children can't walk

safely.

If one of us opens the door for you, we dare you
to become suspicious, but you better look out
cause either we're gonna stab you in the back,
pick your pocket or close the door on your hand
to keep you from fighting back. Cause, like pit bulls,
we now breed our children to fight each other,
kill each other, steal from each other, insult
each other, do anything to keep each other down
in an effort to achieve individual prosperity.

That, for us, is black power and it's also
the reason we don't have any today.

He Touched Me

He touched me
in a forbidden place,
left remnants of
delusion & loathing
in his wake. I was just
a child (inside) so why
did you blame me
for being hurt when
he touched me
over and over again,
knowing that his rough
touching & shoving
would leave me bloody.

I bleed tears
from my eyes; they leave
a scarlet trail that carries
me to a place where
little girls aren't free
to do anything but hang
from a tree
like forbidden fruit
that has been consumed
before its season & even
when you see me
right in front of your face
you know without a doubt,

the essence of me
still hangs from the low
branches of that tree –
within reach, but too far
away for me to ever
be truly free.

Like a zombie,
I stalk the streets
looking for something
to satiate me
though nothing will
ever really fill me up.
I'll always be empty.

A shell of a woman
who's no longer a girl
and all because
he touched me.

What a Black Mother Knows

In loving memory of Trayvon Benjamin Martin and all the other faceless and nameless Trayvons in the world

A black mother knows
that from the moment she
lays eyes on her black son,
the clocks starts to run down.
She has a lot to do to
prepare him for consumption
by the world.

Many a night is spent
with her eyes bleeding tears
as she tries to remember
the recipe for preparing
the African-American male;
'cuz you see today there are more
women raising black sons than men,
but that's a topic for another day
and another poem.

In the beginning the black mother spices her son
with kindness, please and thank you
respect for others, love for his brothers and
a bit of strength to keep her son
from acting like a girl or
being too sweet like his mother.

At the same time
she knows he can't be too brave or strong
'cuz it's way too easy to call a man a monster
when he's wearing black skin.

The black mother knows of the two faces
that will be perceived of her son
and she tries with all her might to
shape and mold each of those faces
while allowing him to maintain his natural identity.

Somewhere along the way,
the black mother tries to add a dose of
independence, hoping it won't be perceived
as negligence
on her part, but you see
a black mother knows
that one day her son
will walk the streets alone
and will need to be able to hold his own.

Black mothers pry their sons' mouths wide
like a bird feeding a baby
to stuff in all the education and wisdom
she has to offer,
filling up her son's insides
with only acceptable spices and seasons.
She adds a dash of compassion and
a trace of kindness toward fellow humans,

while watching as his gut strains against
all the goodness and worth
she has stuffed inside.
She stands back in admiration when
her son keeps it all down; the mother
admires the smooth brown skin
and the stuffing within
knowing that
in the end
his spirit will be carved up and served
to those who stand guard of a cruel and unjust world.
Waiting   waiting   waiting

Never once does the mother tell her son
run from the monsters that stalk
your dreams at night
or the boogey men hiding
underneath your bed;
'cuz we never knew it was necessary
Until mother after mother mourned
the loss of her son right before our eyes
and her son became a monster on trial
for his own cold-blooded murder.
Never once did we imagine
that our son would face a decision
between running for his life and
being perceived as a fleeing felon
Or
confronting danger head on and

being dead.

So the question becomes
How in the hell can a black mother
prepare her son to exist in a world that
only seeks to kill or imprison him?
How in the hell can a black mother
love a son who is only seen as a monster
by those all around him?
How in the hell can a black mother
prepare her son to be successful
in a world that would mentally castrate him
and keep him from being
anything but a felon or victim
of unexplained, but acceptable
violence?
How in the hell can a black mother
be a mother to a son
when it seems
all the world wants her to do
is prep him like a Thanksgiving turkey
and serve him up for dinner?

I'm sorry, what's that you said?
You said I sound angry or maybe even mad?
Well, how would you feel
if I asked you to prepare your son
to be consumed by people
who look at his colored skin,

not seeing the goodness within
or the years of potential ahead,
who only want him dead?

I Hate It

I hate it
when grammy dies,
the one who has
the sweetest hugs and
little old ladies who
smell like moth balls
pinch my cheeks
and say
She's in a better place.
What place is better
than here with me?

I hate it
when stars shine bright
in the sky and brother says
Make a wish sister and
it'll come true. So
I look up to wish for
a brand new Barbie doll
black, if you please,
but I don't get it.
All I get, in fact
is to wake up with a star
on my eye. Nobody says
Don't cry tho
so I do.

I hate it
when Janay is my best friend

in the whole wide world
but
that don't matter 'cuz
mama done lost her job and
daddy done lost his way home
plus there's the fact that grammy's gone
and mama says we gotta move
to the Walter Simmons projects
where there's no Janay plus
grammy's still gone too.

I hate it
when my stomach sings
like a grumbly blues man
who done lost his woman and
I go to the kitchen
but there's no food;
the fridge and cupboard's bare.
The only thing in there is
roaches and a bag of flour
with no chicken to fry.

I hate it
when I rush home
to tell Uncle Pete about
that mean old teacher who
told me I won't be nothin'
in life, how she always
pickin' on me, but he
just smile and his hand
slides up my thigh and
nobody is home to hear me cry

so I just fall asleep
and try to hold my breath,
trying to go be with my grammy
again.

I hate it
when I write a poem
to let people know
how I'm feeling inside,
how it feels to be me
only they don't even care
'cuz I'm not them and
they not me and
that's the way they want it
to be.

**For all the little girls who have a "normal" life that's
anything but normal.

If Hope Were Dope

If hope were dope, I'd
get high off you. I'd
smoke your dreams and
send them back to you
with wings and a small
flame to set those
dreams on fire.

If love were a flame, it
would burn my insides,
consume my inner being,
set me on fire, keep my
desires and your dreams
from going up in smoke.

If peace were clouds
in the sky, I'd seek them out
always. Want to rest in
the shade of the magical
days of us, days where I
can luxuriate in your
presence. Us 2 alone.

If smiles were the sun,
the warmth of your
smile would dry up my
tears, decrease the sum

of my fears. Basking in the rays of the sun of your smile, I won't need protection. SPF 2, will do just fine. Just me and you.

Dichotomy of the Strong Black Woman

To carry the world on our shoulders
without uttering one word of misery,
yet to desire the pearls of womanhood
that is the dichotomy of the strong black woman.

We wear the mask that grins and lies
because we want to hold onto our pride,
then pay the price by being pushed aside
as a way is made for a woman, the real ones.
My black Kings don't hold the door open for me
because I told him I'd do it myself.
My black Kings won't hold their hand out to me
because I told him I didn't need him.
My black Kings won't defend me
because I proved to him I'm a strong on my own.

When the rent is due, I won't call you
or anyone else 'cuz I got this. When
the TV is on the fritz, I'll figure it out
'cuz I got this. When my tire is flat,
I won't call you 'cuz I got this. When
I need help, any help at all, I
won't call you 'cuz I got this.

Somehow the **strong** overshadows the woman
so I'm left standing all alone. And it's those times
when I'm all alone that I take off my mask and

see the lies I've been feeding you and me, that
even though I can handle it all on my own
I don't really want to. And that's the dichotomy
of being a strong black woman.

Africa, To Me

Why am I even here?
The answer found in my tears
is to bear the burden of hurt
and shame. Nothing but disgrace
shines in my eyes. I'm so tired
of hurting; just wanna be free
from the hundreds of years of misery—
slave to a homeland that no longer
recognizes me. Oh, Africa, you claim
to see a majestic Queen when you
look at me, but I shudder to have
to admit that though you are my
birthplace, it is in your arms
I learned to feel a shit stained
misery. Smeared all over my face
your bloody feces – Stop! I scream
yet I accepted it with my eyes &
mouth wide open while proclaiming
you are Africa to me. I open
arms wide, accept the motherland
inside, feel it nestled between
my thighs and I sigh – Home.

Home is where the heart is & also
where it's shattered to pieces.
All you are is inside of me
tryin' to convince me you're a part of me.

Africa you can no longer hear me
and I don't know if you ever
could. Every day I plot to be free,
to break the chains of bondage
holding me tight, tied to a place
that could never love me.

Rhythmic beats once sang to me
opened a NEW WORLD to me.
You promised me, O Africa, to
always be that space where I
could return, but I look at you
& no longer see a place to call home.

Mama always used to tell me
"I brought you in, I'll take you out"
You were supposed to be different
Africa. You're the same, but worse
cause you showed my worth to me
then sent the stocks of me
plummeting. Why Africa!
Don't you realize I always
loved you Africa? I would have
done anything to return home
but now I just want you gone
so you can stop hurting me,
stop pretending to love me
when you don't even love yourself.
If you did, how would you be able

to do this to me? I wanna
return home and wanna be free.
So Africa let go of me.
Our history is now diluted
& watered down and I see
that Africa could never be
home to me. Stop, Africa.
Stop trying to break me.

My Nappy Roots

In the palm of
   my hand
is the sum of my
   bitter history.
It is a history steeped
deep
   with a poisonous
pain that runs deep and
stabs like hypodermic
needles, filling my veins
with
hateful words that are
seeking
to find life again.
Its strong flavor –
a
   shock
to the senses like
a cup of coffee made
from
beans that traveled
on ships,
crossed many seas &
water
filled with bones like
ice cubes in your glass
   of water.

I stop to savor
  what
  it means
to be down there
trapped in the sea --
forgotten.
When I travel
  across
paths created at my own
fingertips,
I am greeted by
a sea full of
griots
who remind me
the rough terrain
I will travel
every day
is
helping me to
build strength
in a place
where
those who thrive
are pissed off 'cuz
black people dare to
survive.
"You ain't s'pose to
be free," they

---

remind me.

You call them
   Maligners,
   accuse them of
spreading lies
but
the truth is
they're
wrapped in my roots
&
no matter how hard
you pull
I cannot, will not
be
free
from
my nappy roots.

An Open Letter to the Man Who Pulled the Trigger

We're tired
tired of ingesting
stories of ur
massive detachment from
civilized society and
ungodly attachment 2
the heartbeat that thrums
its searing message of
hatred and destruction on
our collective soul.

Our collective tears have
finally hardened by the
misdemeanor of ur soul
and ur ungodly actions
have taken their toll
and it's like u've gotten a hold
to us around our cowardly
necks and u
won't let us breathe,
granting us a reprieve from
seeing you regurgitate
the evil bile you swallowed
with ur Lucky Charms this
morning.

But, you see, tired

as we are, we can't
be bothered to fight back
so don't expect us to
waddle out of the negligent
comfort of our Lazy Boyz
in the cesspool of our egotistical
comfort, for we will not be
disturbed, our feathers not
ruffled; we'll simply turn off the news
and continue to refuse to
acknowledge the discomfort of
our souls.

Memories of a Whore

I never walked midnight
streets, but allowed you to fuck
and use me – same difference.

Revolutionary Poet

I've got to make it out the hood alive before I can even dream of
fighting for something bigger than survival.

You want me to share truth with you
like tiny bits of chocolate that must be
consumed before the sweet treat
melts everywhere; now it's just a mess
with no trace of usefulness unless
it's to lick it off your fingers and
that will leave no one feeling full.

You seek a poet who will coddle and
comfort you in the safety of your lies,
one who fails to realize it's not enough
to dry gulch the white man with
evidence of past misdeeds, constantly
holding their foot to the fire
while you lay claim to no responsibility
for what's happening today.

It's not easy being a black poet
when you're not simply restating the truth
that $2 + 2 = 4$, but when you take
that basic knowledge and reveal the larger
problem that $2+2=4a \times 4$ and divide that
by abc   nobody wants to bother with
the algebra of the equation because
it's easier and simpler to stick to the basics.

The disintegration of values in our

neighborhood is the immediate bed
that needs to be made up before we
can talk about failures of integration
in the classroom

The poet's job like the preacher's
is to make you uncomfortable in the sin
of your surroundings, not to use
the butter knife of truth to
sculpt the finger of blame while
inducing societal shame to
offer a crutch of disapproval to
help you limp through life.

Don't consider me less a poet
or less black 'cuz I refuse to
tempt you with dollops of truth
shoved between two blank sheets,
the same sheets used to attack truth
thru the use of ignorance, hatred & abuse.

I refuse to employ the tactics
of the enemy while calling
myself a friend.

You say I'm not a true Revolutionary poet
and accuse me of being less black 'cuz
I wear the emblem of shame across my
breast knowing you'd rather attack
the sheet in which you say I'm dressed than
deal with the true distress plaguing our families.

Don't don the white sheet of shame
'cuz LeRoi walked out the door and
stopped taking care of his kids, instead
be outraged 'cuz his arrest record is four
pages long so the man refuses to give him
a chance to turn his life around, fearing
instead a fruitless ride on a merry go round

and

Don't publicly shame Lakeisha for teaching
her girls to twerk for dolla bills stuffed
in the bra instead of teaching them that
the unfairness of life requires them to gain
knowledge from books and stop worrying so
much about how they look – yeah she a dime chick
but she stupid and don't know shit
except how to make her ass clap, but
what the hell it's clapping for when
intelligence was long ago shown the door
to make way for indentured servitude of the mind
that says we got to grind in the streets and
not in the classroom or that mommy dearest
can't be too interested in raising me 'cuz
she's too young to be a mama and she's just
trying to be free of the responsibility of
motherhood, so she can blame a broken system
in the end... a system that didn't do its job or hers.

Stop getting mad at me 'cuz I chop you
with my words and serve them on a platter
with the tart and bittersweet truth that

Jessie and Al need to take to the streets
while voicing outrage that Malik shows up
to school packing heat, after failing
to show up week after week
with not one sheet of paper nor
pencil or pen, just a rebellious attitude --
hell no, you can't educate me!

We need to sleep in our wailing clothes
'cuz our black men are being reduced to
numbers they can rack up on the floor or
in the field – not to mention numbers across
the backs of our youth who think it's cool
to skip the education offered in school;
it's not palatable or preferable to what's
being taught in the streets.

You say I'm not black enough
when I fail to jump
on the bandwagon of lies that claim
frustration and outrage with what those
outside our race think about us while
shirking the truth that it's us doing
the most harm to us. Perhaps Kobe
is not a traitor, but Ray Ray who gunned down
Pookie is the real traitor & you're just too scared
to admit it even when you see intelligence is
sharper than a kitchen knife and
an intelligent solution can be shot
into the vein of our black culture to turn
things around before we're even more
irrelevant.

It'll takes more than reactionary blackness to fix what's killing our community

Grandma's Shoes

Grandma never was much of a diva, she
was never impressed with material things
and she would wear shoes with the foot
cut open just as quickly as she wore those
brand new from the store.

She was the type of woman with so much
love to give that we always sought her out
when we were feeling empty and needed
filling up. Some say they see my grandma in me.

If love were an ATM, I'd be just like grandma,
cutting the toes out so that the shoes still could
fit; shoes never were meant to last forever.
But love was. Wasn't it?

If my daughters ever ask me what love
should feel like, will I have to tell them
that love doesn't always fit? There isn't always
room for love? Will I say, you'll know when it's
right? "You'll just know." When it fits, I'll say
it'll just feel right and you'll never want to
take it off –like grandma's shoes.

Sugar Ain't Always Sweet

Sugar ain't always sweet.
Sometimes it's something just
to cover up all the bitterness.

Did I deserve to die,
to have my cries go
unnoticed, unanswered, to
fall hollow on deaf ears, ears unwilling
to save me? Why did I deserve my fate
because you tried to keep me safe by
telling me to avoid a life in the streets,
because you stared hard at me, trying
to impart dignity to me, not understanding that
dignity had been stripped away from me
a long time ago. The first time, in fact, that
I felt the need to undress in order to unload stress
of paying my rent, of keeping lights on,
of feeding my children –my daughter and son.

You fling hateful epithets in my face, words that
slide down my face like the saliva of hate
because obviously you fail to see nobody could hate me
more than I already hate myself. The dope that flows
through my veins keeps my head bowed so my eyes
don't rise up to reveal my own inner shame.
With every layer of clothing I peel away,
I pull away another layer of pain inflicted by
my daddy, mother, brother or uncle. But it never
stays put away for long. The time always comes when
I have to put the pain back on.

Somewhere along the way, I learned
to drape on the armor of "Fuck you,
this is my life and I'm making that money!"
but don't be fooled by my hard words and my
hard life. I'm just a little girl inside who always
dreamed of one day being someone's wife.
I'm just a little girl inside, trying to hide away
from all the pain that litters my life. I'm a little girl
who wants to be loved but at the end of the day,
I need to be paid. And those who pay me
to lay down and offer an imitation love act
are just as empty as me and you. So, why not
take the money and run when we're all running
and hiding from something or someone?

The only difference between me and you
is you open your legs wide to accept positive
gratification inside, through work promotions, social
climbing, and kids who excel at school and I open
my legs to accept the pain that broke me
in the beginning, when I was nothing but a little girl.
I wear my pain, made it my badge of shame, while trying
to fight fire with fire, and you, you placed yours on a
shelf in the back of your mind, learned early on that
fire can't diminish fire, only makes it grow bigger, become
an all-consuming blaze that burns your face, your spirit,
your clothes, your hair, and you. Instead you cover
the fire that attempts to consume you with tiny granules
of Sugar cubes. A syrupy sweet cover-up for pain you
learned how to hide. One day I'll let you teach me how
to hide, but until then I got to make money

'cuz the bill collector don't care about the skeletons
in my closet, the ice in my heart, or the pain in my eyes.
So I lay on my ass, close my eyes, open my legs and
welcome pain inside. I hope this time the john only
stabs me with his penis and not the knife he has to
hide for those times when someone tries to unveil
all the pain that he's carrying inside.

*For the woman who was stabbed outside our house and
left there to die. My family and I always wondered what
happened after the authorities showed up. We hope that
you learned to see the Sugar in you, like we did that night.

Untitled

ss me,
ces others
never knew existed.
I love the way
I can hold you while you
hold me and it's impossible
to tell where I end and
you begin.
I love the way
my thoughts flow
into the river of your
feelings and the wind
doesn't have to blow to
reverse the flow, sending
your thoughts coursing into my river.
I love the way
we can be friend and
lover to one another -whatever
we need to be. 'Cuz our love
fashions the way we are
with each other- we uncover
our own masks, love's exposure.
I love the way
the releasing of you
fills me up, keeps me from
feeling empty. Except when
you are away from me.
I love the way
me without you seems an

impossible reality as long as
my memory bank is full. 'Cuz
ours is a love to never be
forgotten.
I love the way
you love me and I
love you. I love how
there's no pretense and
no façade of truth.
I don't have to
shield myself
from loving you.
Because loving you
is the gentlest of sins,
one I confess
over and over again.

I love how I
look at you
and see the plain
truth, that I'll
never be free
of loving you
because we choose
to be free with each
other, knowing that
choice
is the most important
element of love.

The Adopted Child of Emotions

Love is the adopted child of the emotions.
The one we all thought we wanted, but
never could have. Not actually and definitely
not perpetually. So we create clever little pet
names to keep Love from knowing she's the
malformation, an abomination of how love
should be. There's the Love you settle for
'cuz you're tired of being alone. There's
the Love that comes disguised in her Sunday
best, knowing she only needs to pass a
pop quiz, not a real test to be accepted fully.
And, there's the Love that is obsessive to
the extreme and jealous and mean so she
separates you from everyone and everything
you once loved truly. The Love
that makes you feel unworthy to be in her
presence, so you spend year after year, month
after month, day after day, trying to stay in the
game, trying to stay the same while changing , all
in the name of Love. Or the Love that must be kept
a secret, so she hides in the closets under piles and
piles of junk you've collected over the years. Till you
forget she's there or till she finally faces her fears
and comes out to walk away from you.

This adopted child spends too much time trying to
fit in where she doesn't belong. And too many of us
keep welcoming her into our home, though she needs
to be free to roam until she finds
where she truly belongs.

I have a friend who once told me love is not the
adopted child of emotions, but a word people use
to label anything involving any type of emotion. So
Love wears the disfigured face of a foster child who
never should have been adopted. Her heart too
broken, her soul too shattered to love.
But it's only a disguise to hide the pain glistening
in her eyes, a tell-tale sign that love, for most,
is the adopted child of emotions. But,
there are those, like my friend who invite
Love in because love, for them, was born
naturally and love, for them, opens, not closes,
accepts without changing and breathes light
into darkness without announcing her presence.

What If...

What if...

Cinderella never received a kiss?
ignorance really wasn't bliss?
promises weren't sealed with a kiss?
and meeting you wasn't a near-miss?

Always coming close, yet
never quite close enough

What if...

Dorothy never found her way home?
Larenz & Nia never felt a Love Jones?
the Greatest height felt was to the moon
or the flower Narcissus had never bloomed?

What if...

I trusted the promise behind your kisses?
knew that me without you is imperfection,
while the two of us together needs no perfecting?
And the completion of us remains an enigma?

What if...

I'm meant for you and you for me,
but still we have been waiting in vain
and stumbling through the darkness while
the constellation of our love fades away

leaving us both in complete darkness?

How Do I Love Thee –2014

How do I love thee?
Let me count the ways…

I love thee for the way
I never have to pay
whenever we go out to dinner.
I love you for the way
your eyes never stay, for too long,
on our waitress' ass.
I love you for the way
you seem to know all the words to
all my favorite songs – or are they
your favorite songs and that's why
I love them?
I love you for the way
even when you don't have time for me or
too much time to spend with me, there
is no amount of money you won't spend
on me.

Being loved is not the same as
loving, and yet my closets overflow
with things you've bought for me
there's Michael Kors, Prada, Coach &
Louis Vuitton –symbols of your love for me.

How do I love thee?
That's the question you asked me.
And I cannot tell from where the
question springs, but I love thee

for all the little things,
things you do for me, when you
seem not to want to be seen with me.
Or maybe you're just too busy for me.

So I love thee for the words
you whisper to me, late at night,
when everyone else is asleep.
Words are the blood coursing
through my veins, keeping me alive
and those whispered, Baby I love yous
keep me from drowning in a sea of
self-deprecation, self-hate, and self of
the nobody loves me and nobody
wants me.

Everybody needs a place to be
and I've found my place inside thee.
So, if you really need to know
how I do love thee, just look
inside the crevices of your soul,
the dark places you have fortified
with steel and concrete walls
to keep from catching feelings (for me)
and you'll find me there,
curled up in the fetal position, trembling
with anticipation and waiting for you
to finally notice me. And love me.
Like I love thee.

Don't Fall For Love That Doesn't Fall For You

Why do you keep knocking on doors
you know will never be opened to you? Doors
that are blocked by the very men who claim
to love you? Why do you keep watching them
walk away, day after day, knowing their intentions
were never to stay   with you? Why do you stay
and try to force yourself where you don't belong?
Stop, okay, it's not fair to you and you know it.
You should stop and try to see who the real problem
is. It's not the men who end up leaving you.
Everyone loves to pay clearance price for goods
they receive, and he loves not having to pay
full-price for the love you give. Just like the ones
before him, he spotted your clearance tag. So,
again, I ask you why do you keep allowing yourself
to be devalued when you say you only want to
find someone to love you as hard and deep
as you love them? Time after time, you keep choosing
to stay with men who fail to value you in word or deed.

Why do you let him put your heart on a string, like a
big red balloon, headed to the outer reaches of the moon,
alone? He's only stringing you along, staring in detached
amusement as you run along to try and keep up with him
while he plays with your heart, plays with your emotions &
stokes your fears of always being alone. Stop telling him
shit
about how he makes you whole while he gives you no role
in his life. Stay in your lane, the place you belong.

It's time to pull out, let the wasted years trickle to the floor
like children unborn, a love unformed. Once you pull out
of that space that was never meant for you in the first place
you can place your heart in the hands of a man who
won't take your love & loyalty for a broken toy.
Finding love in life is all about choices, and if he's not
choosing to love you, maybe it's time for you to move on
&
replace your love with his potential and what the future
may hold
with that old-fashioned love you used to feel for yourself.
Then
wait for the man who will not only be there to catch you
when you fall in love with him, but he'll fall too &
while he's falling he'll grab hold to you & never let go
until he has you right where he wants you: by his side,
not as a side chick or the other woman, but as the
only woman he wants to come home to.

Suicide Note

I washed the mirror with
my own tears and exposed
my fears. As I wiped the
drops of sadness away, I
scrubbed away the layer
of protection that hid the
truth. I've always been
crying inside and knew how
to hide the tears beneath
a veil of intensely loving others.

I loved you because I couldn't
love myself. Helped you and
never asked for help. I've always
been broken but you didn't know.
I hid behind the shadows of
"Do unto others as you would
have them…"

If, just once, you bothered to look
beyond the facade, you might have seen
that little girl inside who has stood
in the same place, stagnant, year after
year, with tears swelling in her eyes,
a rip tide of grief that couldn't know
relief because she was afraid of letting go
totally.

A little girl who possesses
the kind of sadness that stares
longingly at a bottle of pain
medicine, wondering if the secret
of happy-ness lives at the bottom
of the bottle. Can I? Will I? Can
I? Thoughts that whirl around my head
like wisps of cigarette smoke,
(she thought she was blowing bubbles.)
Doubt paralyzes me and I can only
wonder if the wispy thoughts will
once and for all strangle me,
snuff the life out of me.

I can't breathe when my
throat is full of pain pills
and I can't scream when
nobody is around to hear
me. So I stuff my pain and put
it off again, but I know one day
soon I will have the strength
to dry the tears from the mirror
and from the little girl's eyes.

The Longest Cut

Loving someone opens a part
of you, draws the longest cut
across your soul and leaves you
vulnerable to an ill-formed love,
one masquerading as love reborn,
but it's just unrequited love
to the second degree, the one
that takes out its blade & slices
a deep cut, way down deep to
the bottom of your soul where
it bleeds out life.

Love that begins or develops
from the bond of friends
then matures, carries the greatest
risk of all. For nothing is held
back and nothing protected,
no latex gloves worn or
a cleansing of the skin
to prevent infection. Trust,
the only aspirin taken
to prevent thinning of blood
from the infected love of a friend.

A love that started on a day
when the skies were blue, yet
average and the birds sang, too,

their average melody, and
the words you whispered to me,
I love you, transformed & colored
my existence in an average world
& made blue skies seem bluer
while causing an unraveling, the
pulling away of layers of my soul's
self in order to make room for you.
Yet
over the years, with the gentle-like
precision of a practiced surgeon,
your words sliced me open
like the tip of your blade,
made room in my soul for
the junk science love you made
readily available to me. Hateful words &
slippery feelings of non-worth took root
in a soul that only desired to love you.
Genuine love was replaced with
the bitter root of a lonely childhood,
a seed of remembrance of a time when
stone cold mothers stood sentry to
carefree days of childhood, like troops
awaiting orders to shoot anything that moves.

Where you should have deposited gold,
you shoveled in piles of shit.
Proud of your handiwork,
the clever surgeon with the

magic hands stood back and admired,
surveyed the scene & deemed your work
done and nothing but fun
'cuz – oops, you're not the one
and all great surgeons
require dummies to practice on
so now you lean over her/me/she
and whisper the words "It's done"
and carry on like you're not
Jack the Ripper, slicing and dicing
innocent souls, but
just a surgeon of love
repairing blackened & tortured souls.

Choices

To love me or leave
me hanging from rafters of
insincere love & fear.

Ghost

A silhouette of broken
memories, loves, and dreams, the
death of all fond things.

Moon Dies of a Broken Heart

Blood drips from the moon,
a stab wound thru the heart; he
loved too soon. Death.

She Caught Hell Like a Cold

Damned to a life of
loneliness, she tried to kill
love, hide the corpse. Hell.

Grandma Used to Wear Men's Shoes

Grandma used to wear men's shoes
though she never tried to stand
like a man. Like any woman who
carried love for her family in her heart and
Mother Earth determination to hold her family
close to the security of her love, she just
wanted to be free from having to stand
alone, at the end of the day.

Her hands
were rough from years of picking cotton and
her joints stiff from a lifetime of dropping
her self-respect and self-love on the doorstep
day after day, whenever she'd leave the house.
Always they'd be there to greet her when she
dragged herself home most evenings – sometimes
the neighbor's kids would find them and play
with them until their parents would force them
to return those feelings back to grandma's doorstep.

One day the neighbor's kids - did I happen to
mention those kids were white – took grandma's
feelings and hid them underneath the porch of her
sharecropper's shack and charged her ten dollars to
go get it. That was her last ten and she just slipped
on those shoes that belonged to a man
at some point and walked tall as the strong black

woman she was.

One day a man was standing on her porch, he
was protecting those feelings she had left on
the doorstep. He said he'd spotted her leaving
the field one day and instantly fell in love with Grandma.
That day grandma traded in her men shoes and,
for once, walked like a woman until the day after
grandpa died and she was forced to wear
men shoes again.

This Is Just Another Love Poem

I want to dive into your mind and
swim laps around your thoughts,
skinny dip through your dreams wearing nothing
but the smile thoughts of you bring to my face.
I want to drape my body in only memories
that have made you smile over the years so
your lips curve upward when you see me,
think of me, speak to me, long to be with me.

I want to make verbal love to you,
using only our words to tease to arouse
to seduce one another to the point of
mental orgasm. I want to thread the lines of
our conversations through the tiny opening of
that one in a million chance that we'd meet one another,
use the strands to create a shawl that I will wear always,
to remember the sound of your voice, your words
becoming
fingers that play gently against my skin, stroking me like
the ivory keys of a baby grand piano.

I want to lose myself in your gaze then
find myself lying next to you
on a blanket, underneath the old dogwood tree
in my grandmother's back yard. I'll feed you
green grapes and strawberries from our picnic basket.
I want to bathe in the intense waters of your gaze,
allow each and every wave of your thoughts to carry me
away. I want to climb out of the ocean of your eyes and
dance seductively with you underneath the stars, our feet

wet with sand, our bodies wet with perspiration. Always
I want to look up and see myself in your eyes,
in your future, the one you're slowly walking toward.

Over time the layers have been pulled back
to reveal the gentle waters flowing through your being,
and if it were possible, I would strip naked,
climb on top of you and dive into those waters,
never to emerge again.

I want you, but I can't have you.
I want to sip my favorite wine from your lips,
spend all night taking a dip in your mind.
I want to spend all night lying in your arms, and
the rest of my life lying in your thoughts.
But when I see you tomorrow, I'll just mumble hello
and look away because
she's your wife, you're her husband, and I'm nobody
to you. And this is just another love poem.

Drowning In You

When I look in your eyes,
I want to swim in the depths of you,
trying to catch my breath
before I drown, I feel myself drowning
in you, but please don't try to save me.
I'm right where I want to be.

When you wrap your arms around me,
I want to climb into your embrace, and
come face-to-face with you, the master
of my desire. I want you to nurse me,
nourish me with your sweet juices, and
fill me up with the goodness of you.

When my lips touch yours,
electricity shoots through me,
curls my toes. No, not electricity—
more like a warm whisper is exchanged
from your soul to mine – telling me
that without you, I'm not whole.
And never will be, so please don't let go.

Don't you see how much you
mean to me? This is no infatuation
limited by imitations of what some may
call love. I close my eyes and instantly
I know, I would use my last breath
to tell you once more that I love you.
Though I hope you can see it already,

the way loving you shines brightly
within me. The way I need you constantly.

The question I ask myself: Is it healthy
to love someone so much, knowing
that your gentle touch, or
even the memory of your touch
stirs something within me, makes me
feel things I never felt before
knowing the only option to loving you
this much is to learn to love you more.
I love you more every day and
this love, the feeling that bounds us, one
to the other, is here to stay.
And more than anything, I hope that you
too are here to stay. Forever.

Swimming to Safety

Swimming in memories is a dangerous feat.
Six feet deep in memories of you and me,
I nearly drown as they encapsulate me,
wash me up on abandoned shores of misery
with my body responding to fatal memories
of your yam resting inside of me,
filling me up, touching and destroying walls,
a distant memory; my body folds under the weight
of memory, refusing to acknowledge what I can see,
that when you touched my body,
you failed to touch my soul, didn't even
act like you knew I existed outside what you found
between my legs, spread wide,
welcoming your company,
trying to fulfill my soul needs, empty physicality.
I was too blind to see, you didn't value me &
too lonely to care. Now I just wanna be free
but I don't want to be alone, so I cling
to distant shores, littered with selfish vanity,
hoping one day you'll change and come back to me.

Please don't.

Nothing Feels Certain Anymore

Nothing feels certain anymore,
nothing set in stone. Celebrities

inflate their egos in the foundation of a love struggling
to find its own. Doubt washes her hands in the

space between our deep, exploring kisses.
Questioning presses a palm into the space between

your all too infrequent visits. Disbelief climbs
in and roller skates a path thru your heart,

leaving a trail of bread crumbs behind, an insignificant
treat to entice the icy pain of loneliness.

It's an act of defiance to skate across the Passion
Walk of Fame wearing anything but glass slippers.

And only when you stand back to admire
those cemented hand prints do you realize

that Holly-would is a city of dressed up,
dolled up starlets whose only mission is

to disassemble actuality and introduce us to
confusion accepted as reality and resignation
disguised as love. Is this an act or is it fate

that keeps us questioning the depth of a love

that is trapped in the universe above, searching

for a place to land, knowing in the end that
there might never be a place that's safe for it
to exist.

"Don't leave me, even for an hour, because then the little
drops of anguish will all run together." Pablo Neruda

The Many Faces of Love

The man showed up without invitation
He had a box of goodies, solicitation.

I asked him what he was trying to sell
He opened the box and asked, "Can't you tell?"

In the box were a variety of colorful masks
I asked, "What good are these masks to a
simple woman like me? I attend no parties
and have no one to impress.

He shook his head, gave a wave of the hand.
I can see now how little you understand.

"These are the different kinds of love I have here.
Choose the one you want, have no fear.

There's the love that shows up when it discovers you're
searching, becomes a convenient friend turned lover.

The love that's just words, words that are
fun to say and just roll off the tongue. Words
that in the end mean nothing, it was just a pun.

A paper thin love that leaves nothing
but scars, makes you feel hurt deep within. Leaves

a cut so deep and painful, it never can heal.

The love that will strangle you, the one to try and
convince you it's an embrace, when it only wants to
deceive.

The love that you think is the light you breathe
but it's worth as much as a bad hair weave, will
leave you walking around sporting love that's
ill-fitted for you. The kind you should do without.
And the hand-me-down-love that
doesn't really belong to you. It belongs
to some other who doesn't know they share
love with you. You're both wearing
hand-me-downs and looking like clowns.

All the masks were out on my table and
I looked them over and tried to decide
which of those loves would be the one for me
They were all so pleasing to the eye, colorful
and promised to be true, but then I noticed
a small nondescript mask, too plain to catch
the eye. It was still in the box, in a corner.

What's that, I asked. He
shook his head and said "You don't want
that one. That's the one I've had the longest.
Never have been able to sell one of those.
That's the love that is true. It doesn't look
pretty, doesn't try to be anything but what
it is. You don't have to wonder what type of
love you have when you wear this, cuz

undeniably and consistently it will be true.

My eye was drawn to the colorful masks, the
ones that were so very attractive. I knew I
would look good wearing any one of those
I placed them all back in the box and closed
it. Thank you sir. You're very kind. But I've
decided I don't want to have to choose between
the many faces of love. I'd rather just be alone.

For Some Love is a Four Letter Word

For some love is just a four letter word,
a word that sounds pretty and significant.

But, for me, love is the feeling I have when
I hear your name spoken. It's the feeling I have when
I look up and see you nearby. It's the feeling I get when
I look into your eyes. It's the feeling I have when
your lips touch mine. It's the feeling I have when
your arms encircle me. It's the feeling I have when
you're speaking, I'm listening. It's the feeling I get when
your fingers touch mine. It's the feeling I get when
thoughts of you dance through my mind. It's the feeling
I get when I open my eyes and realize the heart that's
beating
is yours, not mine and the rhythm it's beating perfectly
matches mine because you were made for me and I for
you.

Love is the essence of you and me, it defines what you
mean to me and what I mean to you. We have each
other and that is all that matters. And that's love.

Ode to a Sleepless Night

Sleepless nights spent having
Mental fights with self

Unshed tears or
A bevy of unexplained tears

Alternating between extreme fear
And extreme happiness

Rambling interior monologue
Masked by outward song of glee

Being more real in thoughts
Deeds for naught, I'm alone

Soundtrack to our love life
A blues standard played in reverse

Wrapped in warmth of a turtleneck
The noose will kill if we move too freely

Flying to terrifying, dizzying heights
Together, but somehow I am alone

Carefree and in love
Wall of silence stretches above

Around, within, without
Enclosed in silence when

You want to shout to the world
To shut the fuck up & go to sleep

Finally.

Ode to Another Sleepless Night

My heart is like a boulder
I carry around in my chest;
It hurts to feel it there &
sometimes I just can't breathe.

The pain of carrying the boulder
obscures all the good
I used to see. Now
all I can see or feel is
how the inability to breathe
is slowly killing me.

Temporary Love Thang

ur name drips
   from
     my
      lips
like sweet honeydew nectar
that falls down
    below
     my
      lips
to my chin & I have to trace
my finger along my lips & down
my chin to get the last few drops

every time my heart beats it
sends a Morse code message
2 my brain, saying I will
always seek u 'cuz my heart
knows what no other part of me
does that loving u is motivation
4 evry beat of my heart so if I'm ever
foolish enuff to stop loving u
I will die a little inside
until I'm no more & there's only
the memory of me & u

when u speak I imagine
myself dipping my toe in the
clear depth of ur words

evry time u speak, u give
my life new meaning,
a place 2 B free, a place 2
B me   'cuz I know I can
swim in ur words &
not ever B in danger of
drowning
when I'm lying in ur arms,
I don't think of strength or
even security   ---those are given –
instead   I think of the fluffiness
of the clouds & warmth of the sun
on my skin & I imagine frolicking
in the sky above surrounded by
miles & miles of fluffy clouds
'cuz without a doubt   I know
in ur arms is the closest thing
to Heaven right here on earth

when I'm looking in ur eyes
I wonder if ur mother & mine
were sisters or just close friends
'cuz our souls connected is twins
separated at birth, this I contend,
yet our connection remains the same;
see how loving u has me sounding
insane and u ask me will my love ever
change, baby I need u 2 know
this ain't no temporary love thang

The Blue Notes

Long blue notes echo in my soul
                              whole?
No.   The blue notes invade
my soul, metastasize like rock hard
tumors. Malignant cancer cells move glacier-
like along the line of my spine, till
sitting up straight feels like balancing
the whole world on my back.   Invasive
notes   carry me home
where I crawl into bed, long to die.
Exhale my final breath, one long, mournful, note.

How did my life disintegrate into
a ribbon of jazz notes flowing into
a river of blue notes that close
over my lonely body, leaving it deathly cold?

Letter to a Man I Thought Was a Friend

Beneath your disguise of fabricated lies, I tried
to revive a love that never owned the oxygen to
survive. Staring thru the bars, finally at truth, I
saw you and your lips move to the refrain of
Sugar ain't sweet, it's a substitute, or maybe just
an offshoot of something whose job is to
remove the bitter of a life embraced in the place of
natural sweetness, the flowing free nectar of...
realization that I'm just another Sugar, another
two cent whore whose feelings don't matter and
whose love was nothing more to you than a balm,
a Band-Aid to cover something not quite right in
either of our lives.

Shatter All the Mirrors

In the mirror
I see the truth.

Your warm embrace
and comforting touch
the source of my butterflies
are stolen goods that
can't be replaced like
a broken egg discovered
and moved to another carton.

The same penetration –
a gaze that pierces the
wall I built around my
cold and untrusting heart
also causes the stars to
shine brightly at night or
the sun to burn holes in
dreams left out on the grass
beside roller blades and Barbie
dolls for too long.

Dreams belong in the garage
beside your green
station wagon and
the kids' tricycles.
That's why I choose to
walk away, across the surface
of the moon, barefoot,
so I can travel to the meadow

of no return, the pasture of
discontent. A place I can feel
the tinctures of truth
piercing & ripping my flesh
from the soles of my feet.

How can I keep walking
away when all I want is
to reach down and pull
out what is hurting me, the
thing that keeps me
from climbing over the wall
and running away from
the mirror on the back of
the bathroom door.

Loving You

Am I only loving you
cause I need you
to love me in
return?

If so, then
my love is broken
existing in the
shell of
a woman who has
no idea what it
feels like to be
loved by you or
anyone for that matter.

It's not that I
love you but that I
need you to love
me, but you don't
you said you won't
and you haven't.

So why do I keep
on loving you when
I know it's out of
a need to have
you love me?

Wouldn't it be
so much easier
for me to love me
and
cut out the
middle man?

Loneliness Is...

Loneliness is
an empty and abandoned house.
A place where love no longer lives
but occasionally comes to visit. The
windows are closed, the curtains are
all pulled closed too and all the floors
were snatched up in a hurry.

The occupant
of the house never invites any of
her friends over for fear she will be
judged a lazy housekeeper because
the blind cannot see that the beauty
of the house is not in its physical
appearance, but what's hidden deep
within the walls and down the long,
lonely halls.

A 'For Sale' sign
now sits in the front yard for all to see,
an obvious travesty that will carelessly
transfer the deed of the sad little house
and all its problems to whoever stops
to see it. Someone who will move all
his new shit in, pretending to fix it up
but really he doesn't give a fuck.

He just needs a place to rest
his head. And this is better than

nowhere.

Performing the dance
of mere circumstance and pure happenstance
the old owner of the sad little house will
move to another city and downgrade to
an efficiency. The windows will be open
and the floors will be done. But lying in bed
all alone, suddenly she can see that loneliness
can last forever and love is not a home
that everyone can come back to.

Pieces of You

You took out a knife and sliced
off a piece of your pinkie finger and
handed it to me, the only part you
could offer of yourself to me
'cuz there was just no way you'd
offer your whole self to me. So, I
settled for the pieces given to me.

Pieces of you have floated into my
life, settled into my space like remnants
of food that slowly drop down to
the bottom of your glass of red Kool-aid.
And nothing can make those unsightly
particles attractive anymore. Once

they break away, become pieces, it's
not even fit for consumption anymore.
What once was whole is now pulled
in a million directions, trying to maintain
a balance of imperfection – the imperfect
union of molecules that abrade one another
and yet the crumbling pieces sparkle like gold as
they fall to the floor and suddenly the
pieces are being grasped for with both hands.

There was a time when I thought I
could help put those pieces of you back
together, but now I know better. Now
I know that only you can reassemble
the pieces of you and bring your crumbling

self back to a sense of completion.

For now you offer pieces, a scattering of
convenient portions of time and self,
'cuz change is hard and so is facing your
fears. That's why I continue to
find myself being placed on a shelf,
believing those sweet lies meant for me
and no one else, while you drape yourself
in futility, offering up the best of you
to anyone but me, sometimes to those
who desire to keep you in pieces
because a presentation of the whole you
is not attractive to the one who
only desires to feast on your bones.

Waiting in Vain

I've grown accustomed
to being the lady in waiting.
The role of a lifetime. Always
waiting in vain, while bowing
my head in shame. Thinking,
always thinking, I've changed
the course of the crooked path
laid out for me to travel, only
to find the more things change,
the more they remain the same.

And I wait.

You'll never catch me
waiting in the same spot as before;
that's the one thing that always
keeps changing. But I'll always be
that little girl who watches from
the shadows, the broken train
of men who traipsed through our
living room to the bedroom, wiping
their trashy ass feet across my mother's
heart and face. Her tears drowning in
the bottom of a glass. Her pain too
palpable for me to get pass. Always
looking for a way out, a way to move
past a life that seems destined not to
last or amount to anything worth living.

And I wait.

That little girl
trembling in the dark corners of
my heart is ravenous for a love, but
she just spends all her time waiting.
I see her head pressed against the pane
of the rickety screen door, the door that
never could keep out all the hurt. Still
her eyes shine with innocent hope.
She's hopeful and her hope causes me
to cry, for how can I tell her nothing will
ever change for her. That she'll always be the
fucking lady in waiting. Waiting for
shit to change. It never will though.
She's waiting in vain.

And I wait.

People will blame her,
point the finger of shame,
tell her there's no real power
in the name she's inherited. The
name she was called by her mother
or by all of her past lovers. (There has
to be another name for them cause
none of them ever really loved her.
Did they?) You have the power to
change they tell her with an insane
haughtiness. And like the scared
little girl she is, she cowers in the
corner wishing for change 'cuz
she's tired of staying the same.

And I wait.

The plan seemed
reasonable, a simple exchange
with her pain for mine. I would
go to that little girl and lift her
up in my arms. When I did pick
her up and hold her close, all
I did was cry though. Her sadness
seeped into me and I wanted to
die because I knew I wouldn't
be able to change things for her.
No matter how I tried to convince
her she wasn't the blame, she
stayed the same. Just a little
sad girl waiting in vain. Hoping
things will change. Just waiting
in vain.

Alone, At Last

When the door slammed shut,
shut me off from veracity of a
fantasy that fed my tenuous self,
I heard the shatter of my
thoughts, felt the shatter of my being
as the plexi glass pieces of my mind
fell to the ground, sucked in the vacuum
of gravity – the gravity of what goes around,
comes around. A million, fractured,
and tiny pieces sparkle like glitter,
the kind of glitter not found in
your local arts and crafts store.

Upon closer inspection, I see,
the glitter is the kind with jagged
edges that can turn back on
themselves and me,
slice a hole in your, no,
my mind. Pardon my shift
in point of view. P-O-V. A shift
to keep me from crumbling under
the weight –really the reality – my crystal
stair is creaking and cracking
under the weight of
"In case you didn't already know."

A sharp pain races through
me, my mind so absorbed with
the pain – pardon my refrain,
"Ouch! Oh shit, oh shit, oh shit, oh shit.

This can't be happening to me!"
I laugh at the absurdity of me,
the fool, who thought life fair
when Langston Hughes already said,
"Life, for me, ain't been no crystal stair."

So, why'd I perch, up way too high
on the ledge of the Grand Canyon of
my soul, listening to the echo of voices
crying out from the depth of that solemn hole,
"Get me outta here." Unconsciously, I
bring my hand up to my face, linger on that
space underneath my eye, feel the sprinkling
of tears, a scattering of white dust,
like snow, thick layers of cold, trying
to hide all the pain I feel inside. I try,
I cry, I die. That's my trinity. That's my
Peace. Of mind. Light as a feather,
drifting to the floor of the Canyon,
the opening of my Soul.

Impetuously, I resolve to fold
myself inside the outer covering of
my soul, then to seal the contents
like a letter from an old lover.
You know, the one you keep hidden
in the back of the closet, behind the
memories created out in the open. A shield
for the memories that left you hoping
for a different ending to the
happily ever after story that constructs a
feeling of sailing to the bottom

of your soul. Where it's OK to be.
Alone.

An Ex-Lover Apologizes

An ex-lover brushed
past me today, our eyes
locked and she touched
my arm, held me close once
more with her words. She
told me she was sorry. And I
shook her free once more. Her words
haunted me though, for I
wondered why she apologized.
Was it for the many nights we
sat up talking till we could see the sun
rise? Or the coming nights that we
wouldn't spend together anymore?
Or
did she apologize for the many promises
she'd made to love me forever or
for that one time she told me she loved me
no more? I
should have told her she didn't need
to feel bad and there was no need to
apologize cause I learned that love is
a flimsy apparition hiding under children's
beds, a monster to be ignored…when long ago
my daddy shook the mud off his boots and
used those muddy-less boots to walk away from
me. Whenever I'd see him out somewhere, he
never did apologize to me or never said he was
sorry. In fact, he never said a thing. So, she
didn't have to say it either. The evaporation of
love has never surprised me. Sometimes you

look under the bed and it's just not there. And you just have to go on, knowing one day it might return. So, no disappearing love doesn't surprise me anymore. Now, if she'd stayed here beside me that would have surprised me. And maybe then I'd be the one saying, "Sorry."

i am a sensitive piece of fruit

i am a sensitive piece of fruit
a pear that is easily bruised.
my fruit flesh a corporeal canvas
brushed over with violent slashes of color,
muted hues of blue and green
a dotted landscape of pain
beneath the vivid swaths of color
are where i hide the brown mushy
bruises like the one from where
my ex-husband hit me and
down underneath where no one
can see is the long gash from when
the man who didn't want kids
blew up one day and knocked me to the floor.
i fell down into a bowl of fruit salad,
sitting in the cobwebbed corner – alone.
lost where no one could see me
because no one bothered to look.
spiders, roaches, and other nighttime crawlers
walked all over me, sucked me down
to the core, left nothing behind for me.
and one night a stranger saw me
lying there, he took out a rusted fruit
peeler and started peeling back my layers,
seeking to find the best of me. He
wanted nothing but to drain me of my
passion fruit. one after another people
stopped by for a peak, like tourists, gawking,
trying to get a glimpse of this strange fruit.

The Impossibility of Us

I love the impossibility
of loving you possibly
because loving you
will cause the sun to
shine once more, have
us pretending it will
never storm again when
we both know the
flow of our love is
impossible like
swimming upstream with no arms
trawling for fish in the air
finding gold at the foot of
the stair, instead of at the end
of the rainbow.

I love the impossibility of
our love because even
though, there's a billion to one
chance we'll ever meet
each other, I am fortified by
the possibility, knowing you are
somewhere out there. Knowing
somewhere on this PLANet is my
other, my all too distant lover,
the one who will stare into my eyes and
never ever look away. The one
who will hold my hand and
never let it fall. The one
who wants not just a part of me

but wants to capture my all. The one
who…the one.

I am in love with the impossibility
of the possible meeting of our
hearts because once our hearts meet,
finally, after all these years of being apart
we will again become one, forget we
were ever separated at origination
and you'll embrace me and fold me
back into your being. Unless you
got tired of waiting and you joined
hearts with another. What will I do
then when I've carried around all this
love for you, waiting for the opportunity
to share it with you, give it back to you,
ten-fold, knowing you're the breath
to my soul, knowing you and only you
can make me whole?

My limbs will ache in your presence.
My stomach will swell with regret.
And I will write a poem
decrying the lies they tell when
they say it's better to love and lose it
because it's not. I'd rather be in love
with the impossibility of the possibility
of us, than to live in the shadows of
your love with another. I'd rather wish
you were here with me than to see you
there with her. I'd rather just be in love

---

with the impossibility of the possibility
of us, than to be the fool who's happy
because she loved once, but lost
it all to another.

Love Hangover

If it's possible to get too much of love,
I think I've had too much.

From the very first time he touched me
I knew I'd end up drinking
too much of him.
His gentle caresses &
the intensity of the messages
he relays during our lovemaking
leave me quaking & shaking inside
and longing for more.
Even though I can see the shore
off in the distance
I'm not trying to turn back.

Every time I reach out
for him,
he's reaching right back out
for me.
So it's ever so easy to get lost
at sea
in the deep, wide ocean of our love.

Every part of me responds to him
in ways
that can never be explained.
After loving him fully, I just know
I'll never be the same.
And, hell, I don't want to.

I've got a love hangover
because I've been overdosing
on his love.

This is not a hangover to
leave me feeling bad.
It's just getting too much
of the best love I've ever had.
You know, the kind of loving
that makes you sing the blues
cause you don't want to lose it
and the kind of love that
seems brand new
cause you fall in love
over and over again every day.

Love's Eulogy

The last time I saw love
it sat on the side of the bed
with eyes glazed over to hide
that love was slowly dying inside.

He didn't want me to witness
what I knew instinctively.
His love could no longer sustain me.

There are various forms of love
and it's not true that one size fits all,
but love had no way of knowing this.
So I knew
I'd have to make the final call.

You see, I saw the pall
long before I knew certainly
that this love was no longer for me.
The dark covering of your love
had begun to suffocate me and
it began to fill me with
thoughts of hating you and
thoughts of hating me.
And that's when I knew I was living with a love
that wasn't God-created for me.
So, I started writing love's eulogy.

Though I decided to let love go long ago
it feels like a new testament

for this long ago, did me wrong love song
and I'm not gonna sing that tune no more.

I've decided to take my love off life support.
Not gonna accept artificial loving no more,
love that needs extra pumping and
breathing cause it can't breathe on its own.

In the corridor, I'm surrounded by
well-meaning women dressed in white
who seem only to want the best for me.
I just wonder if they can see how hard this is for me.
Still, they offer words of wisdom
as the weight of my decision continues to pull me down.
"Can't you see," they ask me, "that it's better this way?
You've got to let go and try to move on."
Words that are right, yet still feel wrong.

It reaches a point when love is just existing
and
it doesn't seem to matter if it continues living
or not.
When they start to forget what they've got and
that their love exists alongside your love, then
it's best to just let it go.

In the back of my mind, I'd always known
it would come to this, sooner or later, the
moment would arrive, a decision need to be made.
It didn't happen suddenly.
It was a slow, torturous demise.
Surprisingly, it started with a clearing of eyes—

eyes that were blind so long, it was a relief
to finally see.

Death is not pretty, don't get me wrong,
but, then again, I'd known all along
that the day would one day arrive
& I'd have no choice
but to pull the plug.

Before I pull the plug
I just have to know
was it the 11 minutes you were after?
Okay, 12. I won't flatter myself by
fooling myself into thinking
that the time put in outside of those
12 minutes mattered. If they mattered,
would love have died so easily?
It slipped away in the middle of the night,
and didn't put up much of a fight.

If you're bothered by the tears you see
glistening in my eyes, don't worry yourself
I'm not longing for what I long ago lost.
So, why am I crying, you ask. Well,
it's because death is not pretty even
when it's expected.

Like receiving a cancer diagnosis
you wait on the killer cells to spread
and
when you start to realize love is dying,
you spend days anticipating the inevitable end,

knowing there's nothing you can do to prevent it,
yet wishing it didn't have to kill you inside and
leave you feeling empty, while trying to hide
that while love is dying, you're trying
to keep a friendly façade.

There are still days where
I can't believe love is gone.
I look for him still sometimes.
I crave him too, when I hear a certain song
or when I long to just be held.
In the bed, at night, my dreams
are saturated with memories of my love.
And there are still those days when
I wake to find my pillow damp with tears.
Even though I was the one
who made the final decision
to pull the plug.

I'm so terribly lonely without the comfort
of my long lost love.
And
there are those days when it hurts all the way
down to my joints.
Every movement I make screams a reminder
of the love I lost and then
there are days I feel like
I don't want to go on without my love.

You don't recover from death;
that's an eternal truth.
I won't try to convince you

with empty, loveless platitudes.
It's over. I'm through and
that's all I can offer you.
I gave so much for so long,
but most importantly I loved you
and I loved you hard.
But I give up now.
I'm through.

Please accept my resignation.
Don't attempt resuscitation.
You cannot revive what has already died.

Blues Poem I

She wore desperation around her
neck, like a paper chain necklace
strung with cloves of garlic. Somehow
it kept breaking and falling in her lap.
Her friends kept telling her she needed a
good repairman to knock out the kinks and
figure out how to keep the paper chain from
even falling apart. None of them ever imagined
they could figure out how to repair the damage
themselves. That they were equipped with
skills to perform self-maintenance so they too
depended on the skills of the maintenance man.

Every repair man she took it to smelled
the desperation like sex pheromones made
for dipping their sticks in and they weren't
interested in helping her by fixing what was
broken, instead found a way to profit from her
brokenness. Knowing she'd confuse a gentle
caress with a commitment or see love gleaming
amidst the longing that shimmered in his eyes or
confuse her own unrequited love for something
above and beyond what it really was; it was plain
to see how she could easily confuse stolen moments
under the cover of night as romantic because
no one understands the depth of our love, a love
that can withstand the foul invasion of fumes from
doggie shit that littered the wet grass where he
threw her down on her ass and took what he wanted before
leaving her like he found her before, broken and useless

like the empty drink bottles that littered the field behind
the empty house that no one lived in and that's why they
chose it, a place no one would think to find two people
so in love with each other giving their best to one another.
Fucking. That's all. But, hey, her chain was broken.

The desperate girl never stops looking for someone
to help repair the paper chain of her soul , so she
never feels whole, just convenient, used and shoved
to the side with that old foolish pride that once allowed
her to suffer the weight of being proud of the paper chain
of her abused soul. See, she'd delightfully gesture for
people, trying to get them to see, this is where I've been
hurt and taken advantage of before, this is the scar from
when my dad stood on a chair as his life fled out to the
sea, far away from the shores of responsibility. And this,
she'd point is where my ex-husband stabbed me
with words so cruel, I bled sufferance and tolerability
for years. And look, she'd point happily like a six-year old
girl discovering the magicality of a butterfly pollinating
the blooms of flowers left out in the sun for too long,
this is where I've always carried my capacity to love,
see how it's withered and dirty, a most undesirable space;
well, that's the spot where I live most of the time, it's also
the place where I go to die sometimes, or to sleep, to get
away from
all that hurts me. The thing that hurts most, she'll tell
anyone who'll stop to listen, is that no one
not anybody has ever loved me enough to come and
live there with me.

So, if you ever see the woman wearing the

paper chain strung with cloves of garlic, stop and
listen as she tells the story of the brokenness of
love and how not everyone gets the happily ever after,
and when she's finished speaking, pick up a broom,
any old broom will do and follow her to that secret room
and help her sweep out all the shit that has gathered
in the corners and that has piled up in her soul. Let her
know that soul love is whole love and it's much, much
better when it doesn't resemble the love you get when
tangled in the sheets with the one who won't stay
or running the streets behind the one who's not sure he
wants
to stay. Sometimes it's found in the simple, quiet act of
sweeping.

Blues Poem II

the Ritual of Motherhood begs
an understanding of how pain
can be exchanged for the guise
of pleasure to come, somewhere down
the line. perhaps nine months' time
but for those with broken spirits and torn
pocket books, it takes a bit more time
to collect the dimes to buy the cloak of
happy-ness so those nine months
stretch indefinitely to encompass time
it takes to afford Mother Love-ability.

months are spent avoiding the self-
examination of motives for the self-
inflicted wounds of Motherhood, all so she
can one day be called by the name of
Mommy; the Ritual evolves and in all actuality
revolves around the needs of another. and if
she wants to be seen as a Good Mother, she bears
the pain and will not dare to complain about the
decline in presence of self as one tiny, selfish
bundle of joy singlehandedly wipes out who
she used to be. (BM, before Motherhood;
AM, after Motherhood)
wearing a strained smile, the good Mommy
endures all the pain of seeing herself
erased so fully and shoved into the
pocket memories of oblivion. after all,
this is every woman's dream, right?

the gushing down of fluid brings self-
awareness while dragging along behind it a
bloated bag of intense pain that shoots
through her body like a jet-propelled rocket,
penetrating the wall of possibility, making her
wish for the quickness of death. she doesn't
recognize the death angel stalking the foot of
the hospital bed dressed in hospital scrubs
and a face mask to keep out the melding funk
of the natal pass-ology, the study of how time
evaporates through the admittance of a tiny version
of self as it is snatched down between her legs,
forcing her former self to be placed on a shelf
where old, forgotten, and discarded memories go
when no one wants them or they become too sharp
and pungent for anyone to bear. she's not wanted
any longer, though she's needed, a vessel to bring
forth an arsenal of weapons labeled precious cargo.
after the deed is done, she's released back out to sea, this
done in remembrance of me, the act itself issuing a
sacrificial devaluing of self – the Ritual of Motherhood.

the anchor of her inner feelings fight to loose the remnants
of her soul, but the Ritual of Motherhood is stronger and
keeps her tied to the shore. the expectation that she bear
her new invisibility with the grin of a martyr and that she,
too, will hide within the folds of her new reality
as if though her disappearance was part of the act all along,
an Etch-A-Sketch wiping away destined from the start
the making of a Mother's heart.

jim jones himself couldn't concoct a potion toxic

as the Motherhood Ritual. be wary, then, when jim
whispers incredibly his plan to become your god
and the father of your son to cure the fertility
of your fears that rise from the nursing of a naked,
trembling, child, a child who will eventually suck away
life and affability, leaving only emotional fallibility to
just another soul sucking opportunist who will commit
the crime of aggravated robbery of self, justified by
Ritual of Motherhood.

Automatic penalty: 18 Year Sentence

Acknowledgements

I've said it before and I'll say it here again. I have never written a book alone. I offer my gratitude to my wonderful little family, Jasmine, James, Courtney and Cameron Guy. You guys are the greatest kids a mother could ask for. Thank you for all you have done to encourage me.

I thank God for giving me the ability to create, for giving me a vision that has carried me through many difficult days. I envision the dream at night, but more importantly, I carry that dream with me every day. Every day when I sit down to write. Every day when an idea causes me to pull over while driving so that I can write it down. Every day when I am nudged by an idea, a word, or a line that eventually becomes a story or a poem.

Then there are the kids I didn't give birth to: Raven King and Tracie Brooks. These girls, whew, I don't even know where to begin. So, I'll just say that, as a teacher, it's a blessing to meet young women whose lives you are able to impact. And even greater to have them impact your life in return. We have educated one another, encouraged one another, and grown to love one another.

I would also like to offer my gratitude to Uncle Pete. Though you left this earth a few years back, your words have always stayed with me. You made me promise that when I became a famous author, I would buy you a chocolate colored Cadillac. I'm still working on that, LOL. But I will always remember the faith you had in me.

Over the course of this last year, I developed a friendship that changed me from the very first glance. That friendship has inspired me to grow as a writer, as a friend, and as a human. Thank you LC for your friendship and your encouragement.

I also would like to thank all the readers of my blog, *A Writer's Thoughts*. You all have inspired me through your words of encouragement and by sharing your own creativity with me as I developed my own. The writing community we have created is definitely invaluable.

I am deeply indebted to two-thirds of the indomitable trio, the Three Musketeers. You guys rock. Your encouragement and advice have meant the world to me. Serendipity brought us together, but through love we forged a bond that cannot and will not be broken. I love you as if though we were birthed from the same womb, Sylvia Lyons-Bonner and Vicki McCloud.

And there are many great writers who paved the way for myself and others to follow; reading the work of Toni Morrison, Edwidge Danticat, Bernice McFadden, Paulo Coelho, Dean Koontz, Harlen Coben, Michael Connelly, and so many more, all of you who inspired me to keep at it when I felt like I was getting nowhere.

Last, but certainly not least, I would like to thank all the wonderful people who have supported me in my writing career by purchasing my books. You have no idea how much I value each and every one of you for the contributions you have made to helping me be the person I am today. And there are others, too numerous to name here, but I have your names imprinted on my soul. I will never forget.

Peace & Love to you all,
Rosalind

Made in the USA
Charleston, SC
31 May 2015